lonely planet

LONELY PLANET'S ✈ BEST EVER TRAVEL TIPS

GET THE BEST OUT OF YOUR TRAVELS WITH ADVICE FROM THE EXPERTS

CONTENTS

 PACK LIKE A PRO

🐷 SAVE MONEY

✚ STAY SAFE AND HEALTHY

AVOID PITFALLS

 DO THE RIGHT THING

ENJOY EVERY MINUTE

INTRODUCTION

For a travel geek, the prospect of putting together a book like this is a dream assignment: attempt to distil all the important travel knowledge in the world into 62 individual, bitesized tips.

While making sure they're not too obvious – 'don't sit in the sun until you turn the colour of a lobster' is not much of a tip – there's also a need to avoid topics that are too obscure, so there are no guidelines here on how best to tour the rock churches of Lalibela in Ethiopia, magnificent as they are, or map the backwaters of Pohnpei's lagoon canals.

This is also not a task best approached in isolation. We've spoken to several dozen seriously clued-up travel experts about everything from packing to adventure, and urban exploration to getting the most out of technology, and when you should think about leaving it behind. The aim is to pass on universal advice that you can take with you wherever in the world you go, and whatever your budget. And if we pass on a trade secret or two then we, and we're sure you, won't mind at all.

Tom Hall

PACK
LIKE A PRO

Pre-departure checklist

**Don't leave home without getting
the essentials in check**

Your passport

OK, you've probably thought of this one already, but check the expiry date. Some countries require at least six months' validity. And if you have to renew, make sure you leave plenty of time, especially during peak vacation periods. Visa requirements can also change over time so don't assume it's the same arrangement as before if returning somewhere familiar. You can check if a visa is required at www.iatatravelcentre.com.

Pre-book and save

Book in advance before getting to the airport for parking and holiday money. Even if you do so on the morning of your trip you'll save. If picking up pre-booked currency, take the card you booked with and take note if you have to go to a particular pickup point to get your cash.

PACK LIKE
A PRO

Safety
Read up on your destination for up-to-the-minute issues that might affect your plans. The US Bureau of Consular Affairs (travel.state.gov); Australian Department of Foreign Affairs and Trade (smarttraveller.gov.au); and the UK Foreign & Commonwealth Office (fco.gov.uk) are the best places to start.

Get insured – and 'fess up
Travel insurance is mostly health insurance, which is why the cost increases hugely when you get to retirement age. For it to be effective, every pre-existing condition must be declared, otherwise your policy could be worthless and you could end up with a very large bill. Also check that any activity you're planning on undertaking will be included in the price.

Medical matters
Start with a checkup at your doctor's and dentist – it's far easier to deal with any potential issues before you hit the road. Try to go as far in advance as you can in case you need to take full courses of immunisations before you travel. You can usually get any necessary vaccinations at your local health clinic, though specialist travel health clinics can also be found in major cities around the world.

Discount and membership cards
If you're eligible, obtaining an International Student Identity Card (ISIC) or International Youth Travel Card (IYTC) before you go will save you money all over the place – see www.isic.org for details of both. Travellers of any age will benefit from Hostelling International membership (www.hihostels.com). Senior travellers also qualify for travel discounts with some airlines and for ground transport in many countries. Sometimes flashing an ID is enough, sometimes you need to use a local scheme.

Five tips for travelling light

Doug Dyment, author of OneBag.com, gives his
advice for reducing baggage bulge

1 There's only one real 'secret' to travelling light: a proper personal packing list. It's a contract you make with yourself, a personal pledge that you will never pack anything that isn't on your list. And for most people, such a list needn't include more items than will fit in a single, carry-on bag and is able to accommodate destinations ranging from India to Inuvik.

2 Learn about luggage. Most bags on the market are designed to sell easily, rather than facilitate lightweight travel. So learn about design (shapes, configurations) and construction (fabrics, zippers). You may even discover that the primary function

of a wheeled bag is to support itself, not efficiently transport anyone's belongings!

3 Avoid liquids; they are the bane of the light traveller. Liquids (and gels) are heavy, bulky, prone to leakage (particularly on planes), and suspicious to security. Did I mention heavy?

4 Do some laundry. This needn't be onerous: done properly, and regularly, it should be more like brushing your teeth. With the right gear (travel clothes line, powder detergent, universal sink stopper), three pairs of underwear will take you anywhere.

5 Coordinate your colours. An excellent way to derive maximum use from a modest amount of clothing is to ensure that every item goes with every other one.

The ultimate clothes-packing tip

Learn the art of bundle wrapping with go-light guru Doug Dyment

▶ Few travel moments are more discouraging than having your carefully packed clothing emerge at the destination a wrinkled mess. And there's really only one consistently effective solution. Surprisingly, not that many people have learned how to do it.

▶ The twin goals are to eliminate folding (which creates creases), and prevent garments from sliding against one another (the source of wrinkles). All hail a technique called 'bundle wrapping', the careful wrapping of clothes around a central core object (perhaps a flat pouch stuffed with socks and underwear).

▶ Position easily rumpled clothing (jackets, shirts) further from the core, and more forgiving items (sweaters, slacks) closer to the centre. Secure the resulting bundle against shifting, using the tie-down straps in your suitcase.

▶ Follow the steps and you'll find even that dressy linen outfit can be included in your travel plans.

1 Lay out your most wrinkle-prone items such as long-sleeved shirts, dresses and jackets on a flat surface, face up and on top of each other, alternating them in direction

2 Add short-sleeved shirts and trousers, and then less delicate items such as sweaters and shorts, and keep alternating the direction

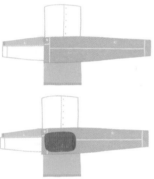

3 When all items are out, add your core bundle, which could be a large washbag, or a zipped pouch of underwear

4 Now start wrapping the items around the central core, one by one, wrapping each item firmly and keeping the fabric taut

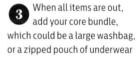

5 When all items are wrapped, place the bundle in your luggage and secure with tie-down straps so it doesn't move around in transit

Backpacker's packing list

**Ensure nothing gets left behind
with our handy checklist**

ESSENTIALS

- [ ] Passport
- [ ] Boarding passes
- [ ] Foreign cash
- [ ] Credit/ATM cards
- [ ] Maps/directions/itinerary
- [ ] Guidebook material
- [ ] First aid kit
- [ ] Travel insurance documents
- [ ] Repeat and travel medication
- [ ] Folder for all documents
- [ ] Large backpack
- [ ] Small combination lock

ELECTRONICS

- [ ] Camera and charger
- [ ] Mobile phone and charger
- [ ] Tablet and charger
- [ ] Headphones
- [ ] Plug adapters
- [ ] Headtorch and batteries
- [ ] Waterproof pocket camera
- [ ] Back-up hard drive

CLOTHES

- [ ] Light jacket
- [ ] Waterproof coat
- [ ] Light jumpers
- [ ] Thin hoodie
- [ ] Casual shirts
- [ ] Vest tops
- [ ] T-shirts
- [ ] Loose trousers
- [ ] Leggings
- [ ] Shorts
- [ ] Skirts
- [ ] Dresses
- [ ] Sandals
- [ ] Flip-flops
- [ ] Trainers/ comfortable shoes
- [ ] Belt
- [ ] Thin socks
- [ ] Underwear
- [ ] Sleepwear
- [ ] Sun hat/cap
- [ ] Swimsuit
- [ ] Sarong/shawl
- [ ] Hidden zipper belt

PACK LIKE
A PRO

COSMETICS

- [ ] Suncream and aftersun lotion
- [ ] Body lotion/moisturiser
- [ ] Insect repellent
- [ ] Deodorant
- [ ] Perfume
- [ ] SPF lip balm
- [ ] Razor and shaving cream
- [ ] Shampoo and conditioner
- [ ] Soap/body wash
- [ ] Toothbrush
- [ ] Toothpaste
- [ ] Make-up and remover
- [ ] Hairbrush/comb
- [ ] Hair products
- [ ] Disposable wipes
- [ ] Sanitary products
- [ ] Nail file/clippers
- [ ] Tweezers
- [ ] Bug spray
- [ ] Laundry kit: travel detergent, braided clothesline, sink-stopper
- [ ] Hand sanitizer
- [ ] Dental floss
- [ ] Small tubes for liquids
- [ ] Tissues

MISCELLANEOUS

- [ ] Painkillers
- [ ] Glasses
- [ ] Contact lenses and solution
- [ ] Travel journal and pen
- [ ] Books
- [ ] Sunglasses
- [ ] Waterproof watch
- [ ] Beach towel/ quick-dry towel
- [ ] Waterproof bag
- [ ] Water purifying bottle
- [ ] Sleep sack
- [ ] Earplugs
- [ ] Refillable bottles
- [ ] Travel neck pillow
- [ ] Playing cards
- [ ] Pocket sewing kit
- [ ] Sleeping bag
- [ ] Portable stove
- [ ] Cutlery
- [ ] Bowl/cup

Travel gadgets

Techy kit that will turbo-charge your trip

As part of the research for this book we asked a host of experts to recommend their essential bits of kit they couldn't travel without. Some things came up again and again...

▶ Tablet + USB keyboard = a computer that can be carried lightly and used anywhere.

▶ World plug adaptor with multiple USB ports – the power junkie's dream come true. In seconds, every drained gizmo can be recharged.

▶ A portable hard drive to back up your photos and videos will take up next to no space and offer an alternative to uploading to the cloud if you're low on memory or away from a fast wifi connection.

▶ Noise-cancelling headphones – perfect for those noisy bus journeys and for any on-the-road video editing or writing undisturbed. A headphone splitter offers you and a friend the chance to watch the same films together on long journeys.

▶ A smart or sports watch can track your distance, location and even provide weather and other alerts, which can be fantastic if you're trekking or cycling long distances.

▶ A portable power source, such as those made by Powertraveller (powertraveller.com), to make your equipment batteries go further. The technology driving these chargers continues to develop quickly. Solar-powered models offer an obvious benefit if going to more remote locations.

▶ Unlocked smartphone. Having a local SIM card can make your life on the road a lot easier, while providing an extra degree of

PACK LIKE
A PRO

GET IT COVERED

Make sure your travel insurance contains dedicated gadget cover if you're going on the road with any serious hardware – and check the excess on any claims for loss or theft. It also goes without saying that you should use hotel room safes to secure valuables.

connectivity and safety. But you can't use one, or do much with it, unless you have an unlocked smartphone.

▶ Similarly, if you use your phone a lot – and, really, who doesn't – a phone case that contains an additional charging unit will give you some peace of mind that you won't be left drained of power.

▶ Travel hair-dryer and iron – small, folding, light, and the best ones offer a variety of voltage. Fewer and fewer hotels and even fewer homestays offer an iron as standard, so if you need to be crease-free, bringing your own is the only foolproof option.

▶ Compact travel binoculars. Not sure if you need them? Try them on your next trip, and see how popular you become as well as how much interesting stuff you spot.

▶ Rechargeable head torch. An unbeatable camping accessory that will make life better on any expedition, or even in a pitch-black hostel dorm.

▶ Something to stand your camera or phone up while you take a steadier shot, like the Gorilla Pod (joby.com/gorillapod-tripods)

▶ Travel scales. Avoid airport repacking scrambles and excess baggage charges by knowing exactly how much your bag weighs before you check it in.

International plug sockets

Here's a run-down of some of the world's plug sockets and fittings

Destination	Plug type	Compatible with others
US	A, B	A
Canada	A, B	A
Thailand	O	-
Australia	I	-
New Zealand	I	-
UK and Ireland	G	-
Europe*	C, E, F	C, E, F
South Africa	M	-
China	I	-
Singapore	G	-
Malaysia	G	-
Japan	A, B	A
Brazil	N	C
India	D	C, D
Israel	C, H, M	-

* Except:
Switzerland and Liechtenstein (type J, compatible with C)
Denmark (type K, compatible with C)
Italy (type L, compatible with C if socket is 10A)

Old school tech

Hi-tech gadgets aside, spare some space for old-school essentials that you never knew you needed

Sarah Baxter, travel writer, editor and author (@sarahbtravels), swears by the Casio F91-W watch. 'For $20 you get a watch that works for ages, has an alarm clock and simple light and, as it looks like it's straight out of 1981, will probably never be stolen. It's an absolute travel classic.'

Baxter also swears by packing a small bag containing safety pins, rubber bands and even an old pair of tights. Find room for a roll of duct tape too. Armed with these you can make on-the-go repairs, pin clothes and curtains and make a crude yet effective seal.

Don't assume you need high-tech clothing. 'You just need to be comfortable and wearing something quick-drying, unless you're doing something specialist like rock climbing or hardcore jungle trekking. Save your money for when you're on the road and need it.'

POSTE RESTANTE LIVES!

One of the great thrills of travel, especially long journeys, used to be picking up a pile of post from home. Despite the growth of the internet Poste Restante (French for 'post remaining') remains an international system for remote collection of post.

This can be done in most locations worldwide, even small ones. In many cases you'll be picking up your mail from grand central post offices, though for the most fun try getting mailed in obscure locations.

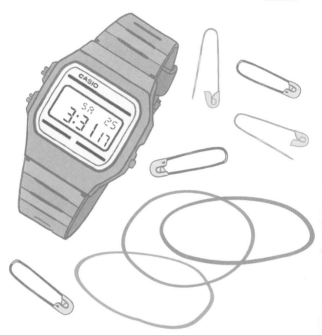

Travelling minimalist but like to be a little smarter on occasion? Make yourself feel a tiny bit more glam in an instant with a few lightweight items: a tinted SPF lip balm, dangly earrings, a light scarf (also useful for keeping warm/keeping the sun off) and a Travalo (a lipstick-sized perfume atomiser).

Hiking in hot, humid climates? Consider a golf umbrella. 'On a recent walking trip to the Caribbean this proved a godsend,' says Baxter. 'It rained, frequently, but the temperature was far too hot to put on a waterproof. The big umbrella also doubled as a walking pole.'

SAVE MONEY

Budgeting tips

Whether you're touring boutique boltholes or backpacking, here's how to make and not break a budgeting plan:

▶ Before you go, work out how much you think you'll spend, then add a little for the first few days. More costs are incurred at the start of a trip as you get your bearings and settle in.

▶ Use available technology: online banking, SMS alerts and apps like Trail Wallet all help you keep a close eye on expenditure.

▶ Try a pre-loaded cash card like FairFX. That way you can only spend what you have.

▶ Look for chances to save money but still get great experiences. Lunch can be a great time to eat out and take advantage of the

better-value set menu deals. In the evening happy hours are also worth looking out for. But...

▶ Consider limiting alcohol – not only will daily boozing add up over even a two-week trip, but when you've had a few you're also more likely to lose control of what you're spending and throw caution to the wind.

▶ Get yourself a prepaid Mastercard from digital banks like N26, Monzo or Revolut – besides fee-free purchases abroad, these alternative digital banks often offer free (but not unlimited) cash withdrawals abroad, plus the option of transferring money at the best currency exchange rates. Check each operator for specific conditions.

▶ Visit countries where you get the best bang for your buck. Your money will go much further in countries like Thailand, Cambodia, South Africa and Uruguay.

▶ Always go local. This puts money into the local economy and also can be significantly cheaper.

Kash Bhattacharya, The Budget Traveller (budgettraveller.org)

SAVE MONEY

The best time to book flights to get the best rates

FAQs for beating the system

When do tickets go on sale for flights?
Usually, 11 months in advance. Reasons for this are arcane and historical – in the days of printed seat plans, airlines wanted to avoid booking people on to the right plane on the right day but in the wrong year.

So should you charge in and book almost a year ahead?
Not normally. Airlines can (and often do) update fares every hour using complex algorithms. This is the dark art of yield management – trying to get full planes with passengers paying as much as possible for every seat.

So when is the best time to book?
There are certain broad trends: on average the best time is five weeks before travel. If you have time, it can pay to watch your route carefully and educate yourself about when cheaper seats are generally available – varying the day of departure and time of day can make a big difference.

What about if you're flying at a very busy time, like over Christmas?
This may be the time to book very early: all fare classes will be available and you should score a price that won't be beatable nearer the time. You'll also ensure you get a seat on the plane you want.

Filip Filipov, head of B2B, Skyscanner

How to bag a bargain in an airline sale

Always get the best price on an airline seat

When the need to fill seats meets the recent explosion in capacity on key international routes – driven by recent expansion by Middle Eastern and Chinese carriers – passengers can, by following a few suggestions, pick up great deals on seat sales.

1 'As a general rule, carriers will have a January sale and a September sale,' says Stuart Lodge from roundtheworldflights. com. 'Airlines are trying to fill seats for the next "shoulder season" – March to May for the first sale, and October and November in the second. Sales aren't unheard of outside this time, but they're certainly less frequent.'

2 If you're travelling during school holidays or other peak periods, there's no point waiting for a sale – you just won't get the deals.

3 By definition, seat sales target routes with sluggish sales. A high-demand, low capacity route is less likely to feature in a sale.

4 Airlines often follow each other's lead in sales, which can cause domino effects in discounting. It's not unusual to have half a dozen airlines on sale at once.

5 Sign up for email alerts and social media accounts from airlines to find out about sales. This is generally how airlines announce sales.

The truth about flight upgrades

**How to maximise your chances
of getting that mythical upgrade to first class**

Getting an upgrade to a superior cabin on a flight is a bit like getting rid of hiccups – there are dozens of colourful theories for doing it, but no foolproof solution. In truth, the only trick isn't really a trick: you've got to work on your status.

'In the event of cabins being overbooked, the decision is in the hands of the gate crew,' says Tom Otley, Editorial Director at Business Traveller. 'They can see the details of the tickets you've booked, and how many loyalty points you have. If you're a regular traveller, and have higher status than other passengers on that flight, then you get the bump up.'

That, then, is the unromantic truth. There remains, of course, no harm in flashing those baby blues at check-in. Where there's a spare seat in F, there's always a chance.

TAKE THE BUMP

Getting upgraded is a perk, but a more lucrative tweak to your journey is being bumped off an overbooked flight – often in exchange for vouchers, tier points or even cash and a hotel room. For those with a flexible itinerary, it's a great way to recoup some of the costs of your trip. If you're waiting to board a flight and hear offers of compensation to those willing to take the bump, position yourself by the desk so you're best placed to swoop in and grab the goodies.

Tips for getting the most from a round-the-world airline ticket

Make the most of the biggest ticket you can buy

A round-the-world (RTW) ticket is a multi-stop ticket covering multiple destinations across several continents. Generally you're on flights operated by a group of airlines that comprises one of the big airline alliances.

Decide when
Travel between mid-April and June to get the best prices, or at least avoid peak travel times – July, August, December and January. By travelling east to west at this time you'll also follow the best weather around the world.

Decide where
Most people structure their trip around two or three of their must-see destinations. Be aware that adding South America generally adds complexity and cost.

SAVE
MONEY

Know the rules

Most people make several changes after their initial booking. Flexible tickets cost more at purchase, but will save you money in the long term.

Know when not to use your ticket

Some countries, such as Indonesia and many places in South America, are popular without being well served by RTW tickets. In these cases it's cheaper and easier to get to a nearby hub and hop on a low-cost flight, then re-join your RTW later.

Land ho

Open sections of RTW tickets allow for a mammoth train ride to see the world from ground level. If you're finding the trail well worn, deviate from the norm by drawing a 'V' rather than a straight line between A and B.

Stuart Lodge, roundtheworldflights.com

First-timer tips for private lodging

Save on accommodation by renting an apartment, spare room, sofa or even a tree house

The world of accommodation has got a lot bigger with the advent of online (and mobile) booking services for privately owned spaces. For first-timers the choice can be bewildering.

Travel writer Andy Murdock explains that it's key to know what you're getting before you go to avoid any unpleasant surprises. 'In many cases, a host is inviting you into their home. Other times, the rental is handled by an agency listing a standard vacation rental. Each experience will be very different.'

Just because a calendar looks open, it doesn't necessarily reflect reality, Murdock explains. 'Hosts aren't always fully on top of their calendars, and they will often want to ensure there's a good fit before accepting your booking. Whether you're talking about Airbnb, Couchsurfing or any of the social accommodation communities, you should have a proper profile on the site that shows who you are, and be sure to tell the host what brings you to town.'

Murdock also recommends opening up a dialogue before booking. 'Ask any questions you need. This back-and-forth also helps build confidence on both sides.'

Picking your first rental
The more you use private lodgings, the better you'll get at picking places that are right for you. For your first foray, be sure to choose somewhere that has experienced hosts and has been well reviewed.

"Whether you're talking about Airbnb, Couchsurfing or any of the social accommodation communities, you should have a proper profile on the site that shows who you are, and be sure to tell the host what brings you to town."

Pay close attention to location. Private homes are often some distance away from main tourist sites. This can be a huge positive, giving you a local's view of a city often missed by travellers, or it can be a huge headache. Understand the lay of the land before booking.

Budgeting

Pricing will vary, but, in terms of value, bear in mind that private homes often come with features you could never find (or afford) in a hotel: full kitchens, multiple rooms, laundry facilities, free internet access. You'll also pay a premium to have the place to yourself versus sharing with the host or other guests.

The ability to self-cater can be a huge money saver, particularly on longer trips. It's also a great way to learn about a city or neighbourhood – a visit to a local grocery never fails to be interesting.

Local politics

As private rentals have become more popular around the world, some cities have welcomed the new options for travellers, while others – particularly large cities with limited housing – have pushed back. Be aware of the local policies before booking a room.

How to get the best deal on a hotel room

Navigate the dark arts of hotel room pricing to your advantage

Hotel prices are so much more transparent these days – online comparison sites do the haggling for you – but there are still some things you can do yourself.

▶ Many hotels, especially private ones, still work on a block-booking system for tour operators, holding allocations that may be unconfirmed. These are usually released 24 hours prior to arrival, so a last-minute deal can be possible if the hotel suddenly finds that it has a lot of unconfirmed rooms to sell.

▶ Someone else's no-show can work to your advantage. The magic hour is 6pm, when many hotels will re-release rooms that haven't been taken, especially if they have not been guaranteed with a credit card. Checking after this time for a last-minute deal can often yield results.

▶ Look out for advance-purchase rates. These are often available 21 or 28 days in advance, but conditions can be quite strict.

▶ An empty hotel room is one of the most perishable items on the planet. The hotelier has one night to sell it and then that night is gone forever so the later it gets, the more chance you have of twisting someone's arm: your something is better than their nothing.

▶ Arriving late may not be the worst thing in the world, especially if you phone ahead to confirm you are coming. As rooms fill up you might find yourself upgraded to a better room.

▶ Hotel chains and big brand names do not like to offer discounts as their pricing is often managed by a centralised team, targeted at achieving high revenues and maintaining brand pricing. However, one way around this, in times of low demand, is to work with a flash sale operator (such as Secret Escapes or Voyage Privé). They will sell off rooms cheaply in hidden deals, which may only be available for a short booking window. The hotel is often not named to protect the brand. Of course there is no guarantee that your allotted 'Four-star central London hotel' is a major brand, but it is a good bet.

▶ Online comparison sites will only check other online booking systems. They don't usually check the hotel's own website, which, particularly with no-chain hotels, often have better deals available for direct bookers, particularly when they are offering packages with add-ons.

▶ Join the club – most hotel companies have loyalty programmes which are free to join. Some can be joined from the brand website, while others require you to sign up when you check in for your first stay. Check out the deals they offer – multiple stays can earn points giving free stays or upgrades, while some offer a discount when you book directly online (eg Accor) using your membership number.

Robert Dee, Hospitality Consultant (robertdeeassociates.com)

Avoid the solo surcharge

Avoid having to fork out for a single supplement by following these handy tips

Negotiate

If you're booking at a time when the hotel or tour is unlikely to be sold out or it is offering special deals, contact the operator to ask whether it will waive the single supplement – it just might.

Travel in the low or shoulder season

You will have more bargaining power outside the destination's high season. When hotel occupancy is low, operators are often more willing to give you a double room for the price of a single rather than miss out altogether.

Book with a specialist in single holidays

These operators may offer the option of sharing a room, or having a room to yourself, for little or no extra charge. As an added bonus, your tour mates will also be solos. Exodus Travels (exodustravels. com) offers solo departures for its most popular tours.

Consider sharing a room

Many operators offer to match you up with another traveller of the same sex to share a room. More than half the passengers who travel with Intrepid Travel (intrepidtravel.com) and Contiki (contiki. com) are solo travellers, with both companies offering the option to match you up with a roomie. Best-case scenario, the operator isn't able to pair you up and you get a room all to yourself for no extra charge.

See Lonely Planet's Solo Travel Handbook *for more detail, and a host of other practical tips for the solo traveller*

Fancy a home swap?

Take the live-like-a-local ethos to the next level, by exchanging homes

One long-standing travel secret is to swap homes with another family, couple or individual. It's a great way to get a feel for local life and save money.

What is home swapping?
Home swapping is different from other ways of travelling. As the name suggests, it involves exchanging your home with someone else's. In its simplest form, you come to mine and I come to yours, so it's a bit like online dating for homes. The concept has been around for a long time and has its roots in teacher and expat networks. If you've seen 2006 romcom *The Holiday*, which prompted a mini-boom in home swaps, you'll get the idea.

> "It's a bit like online dating for homes. The concept has been around for a long time. If you've seen the 2006 romcom *The Holiday*, which prompted a mini-boom in home swaps, you'll get the idea."

Home-swap networks tend to have a membership-based model. Paying an annual fee allows you to swap as many times as you like. This opens up a whole bunch of amazing places to stay around the world.

There are three main groups of people who home swap: families, who love the benefits of staying somewhere different that will have outside space, home comforts and facilities; empty-nesters with time on their hands to explore new places; and business travellers. All appreciate the chance to stay in a home away from home in an interesting part of town.

Making connections

Choosing the right place to stay works in the same way as booking other types of accommodation – you read up about the property, its neighbourhood and the experiences of others who've been there. Unlike other types of accommodation, though, there's a chance to strike up a connection with your hosts as you're in their home and they're in yours. Not only does this mean that you can make friends, it also suggests that mutual respect – and a desire for good reviews – ensures that each property will be well looked after.

Preparing your home

Your own home only needs a few things for it to be ready to be swapped. It should be clean and tidy, with fresh bed linen and towels and, generally, some food and toiletry staples left for those coming in. Beyond this, people understand they're not staying in a hotel and appreciate that every home is different. That said, you should be clear about any specific details, such as if a cleaner is coming in and on what day, and when the bins need to go out – just like you would at home!

Ben Wosskow, managing director, Love Home Swap
(www.lovehomeswap.com)

Claw back the cost of your trip

Take the chance to reclaim those all-important pennies

The silver lining on that missed flight
You may not be able to get a refund on that budget airline flight you missed, but you can reclaim the tax on any portion of a journey you haven't taken.

Maximise loyalty schemes
Make sure you're signed up for and using airline and hotel loyalty schemes at every opportunity, including seeing where you can claim points for additional purchases like car hire. Making large purchases on a credit card that offers airline loyalty points is a great way to pile up the miles – but always check terms and conditions carefully.

Recoup on purchases made abroad
Depending on where you are, you can usually claim back certain taxes paid on purchases made while travelling, especially if you've

SAVE MONEY

paid with an overseas credit or debit card. Check out the regulations for where you're going and where you've been, as there will be forms to fill in (that you can usually pick up at point of purchase). Payment for services such as car hire can't generally be claimed back.

Know the inside track

As odd as it sounds, check if certain elements of your holiday are tax deductible, as they may be if, for instance, you combine a holiday with a business trip. Your home government should have advice online.

Don't lose out on leftover currency

While the exchange rate for repatriating your leftover holiday funds into your own currency will be poor at departure points, you can often find zero-commission fees back at your point of purchase. At larger hostels you may be able to strike a deal with a fellow traveller – if legal to do so of course.

STAY SAFE
& HEALTHY

Malaria around the world

It pays to know where in the world malaria
can be transmitted

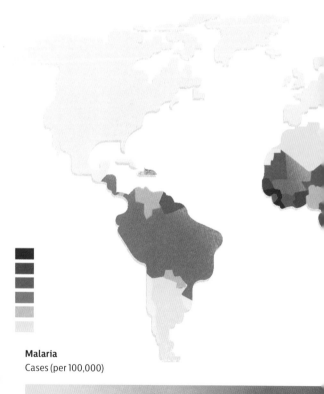

Malaria
Cases (per 100,000)

<10   10–100   100–1000

In some specific areas the risk is reduced at certain times of year.
If you think you're going into a malarial zone speak to your doctor
or travel health professional about the right preventative medicine.
After that, take steps to avoid getting bitten once on the road.
See p48 for advice on staying bite-free.

Source: WHO

| 1000–10,000 | 10,000–25,000 | >25,000 |

Stay healthy while travelling

While mishaps are inevitable, there are simple ways to reduce the risk of sickness and injury

Avoid bites
Whenever and wherever you travel in the tropics, cover up, use lots of insect repellent, and protect yourself from bites during the night using plug-ins, mosquito coils and/or a mosquito net.

Don't expect to avoid common complaints
Pack a medical kit to help you cope with common ailments like cold, flu, headaches, allergies, diarrhoea and indigestion, not just with tropical ailments in mind.

Be mindful of risks
Remember that enjoying the nightlife, sports, swimming, cycling, diving, and using a moped or motorbike may be more dangerous than at home, and the medical care poorer. Prevention is everything!

Stay in touch
There's a big choice of medical guides to consult if problems arise. There are email- or SMS-based systems that can send you alerts about new risks while you're on the road. It is also easier than ever to stay in touch with your own doctor or travel clinic if you need medical help while away.

Wash your hands
Wherever and whatever you eat, always make sure your hands are clean – carry a small bottle of hand sanitizer to use before handling food.

Dr Richard Dawood, Director of the Fleet Street Clinic (www. fleetstreetclinic.com) in London and author of Travellers' Health: How to Stay Healthy Abroad

STAY SAFE & HEALTHY

First aid kit

No one plans for holiday mishaps, but it pays to be prepared with some first aid items

- [ ] Any prescription medicines, including malaria prevention if necessary
- [ ] Paracetamol or aspirin for pain or fever, as well as an anti-inflammatory like ibuprofen
- [ ] Antidiarrhoeals for those long bus journeys
- [ ] Oral rehydration sachets
- [ ] Antihistamine tablets and cream for allergies and itching
- [ ] Sting relief spray or hydrocortisone for insect bites
- [ ] Sunscreen and lip salve containing sun block
- [ ] Insect repellent (DEET or plant-based)
- [ ] Motion sickness remedies
- [ ] Water-purifying tablets
- [ ] Over-the-counter cystitis treatment
- [ ] Aloe vera for sunburn and skin rashes
- [ ] Sticking plasters of various sizes
- [ ] Antiseptic wipes
- [ ] Tweezers to remove splinters and ticks
- [ ] Bandages, scissors and safety pins
- [ ] Blister kit

Beat jetlag

Dr Richard Dawood, Director of the Fleet Street Clinic in London, gives his advice

Any long journey can be stressful and exhausting, with sleep loss, physical discomfort and disruption to eating and drinking patterns. On top of this, you are surrounded by strangers, some of whom may be unwell and passing on their germs. The key to planning a long-haul journey is to keep these factors to a minimum, and to travel with as much comfort, convenience and lack of disruption as is practical or affordable: sometimes it is very hard to achieve the right balance!

Then there's the impact of crossing time zones rapidly, which causes fatigue and sleep disruption in an entirely different way. Correctly timed exposure to daylight or bright light can help you adjust faster to your new time zone. Melatonin has also been shown to help, with a small dose taken at bedtime.

It's perfectly reasonable to talk to your doctor about using short-acting sleeping pills to reduce sleep loss: you can use them to

initiate sleep at a normal bedtime. There are also newer prescription medicines (such as modafinil) that can improve alertness. Medicines don't change the pace of adjustment to a new time zone, but will at least help reduce fatigue and sleep loss.

Travelling with a gluten intolerance

For those with coeliac disease, getting gluten-free food isn't an option, it's a necessity

22

Choosing a destination

Travel writer Anita Isalska (www.anitaisalska.com), who herself follows a gluten-free diet, advises prioritising a destination on the local understanding of the condition and availability of the right kinds of food. 'Italy, for example, has a high level of coeliac testing in children, so diagnoses and awareness are high. India, where chickpea and rice flour are used in many dishes, is another good choice, though naan bread is generally made with wheat flour.'

Be aware of local customs

There are pitfalls to look out for in many parts of the world. 'Soy sauce often contains wheat,' says Isalska. 'Many dishes around the world come sprinkled with breadcrumbs and rolled in flour, so make sure you're clear when ordering.' That said, many delicious specialities including French *galette* (buckwheat pancake) and Ethiopian *injera* are both usually made with gluten-free flour, though you should always check.

Come prepared

Checking, Isalska advises, means 'confirming and double confirming ingredients and travelling with a card explaining your dietary needs in the local language.' She also advises taking a stack of gluten-free snacks for emergencies wherever you're heading.

Fitness hacks for travellers

**When there's no time, no room or no gym
for that big workout**

Physio Katherine McNabb (bodyfixphysio.co.uk) suggests a few
exercises that can be done in hotel room or airport lounge.

Hip flexor stretch
▶ Kneel on a towel on one knee, with the other leg in front, with the
foot on the floor.
▶ Squeeze your bottom muscles and gently push the back hip
forward to stretch it.
▶ Swap sides and repeat.

Neck stretch
▶ Sit up tall and tuck your chin in.
▶ Without turning your head, use your hand to pull your head to the
side and stretch the neck muscles.
▶ Make sure your shoulder doesn't rise up. Hold for 10 seconds.

Reach and bend
▶ Reach up with one arm and really stretch as much as possible
▶ Gently lean over to the side to increase the stretch.
▶ Hold for 10 seconds and repeat on the other side.

Calf stretch
▶ Put your hands on the wall with one leg behind the other and your
feet flat.
▶ Now pull the arch of the foot up – imagine there is a strawberry
under the arch and you mustn't squash it!
▶ Keep the back knee straight and gently bend forward to feel the
pull in your calf. Don't let your arch flatten as you hold the stretch for
10 to 20 seconds.
▶ Repeat on the other side.

Bridging
▶ Lie on the floor with your knees bent and feet flat on the ground.
▶ Rest your hands on the front of the pelvis, then lift your bottom up and hold. Imagine a spirit level staying perfectly balanced across your stomach.
▶ If this is easy, lift one leg straight in front while holding your bottom off the floor. The trick is not to wobble or twist the pelvis.
▶ Hold for 10 seconds, then repeat on the other side.

Superman (aka Table Top)
▶ Get on your hands and knees with your hips over your knees and your shoulders over your hands – just like a table.
▶ Slowly lift one leg out straight behind you and lift the opposite arm out in front. Try not to wobble or twist your back, and make sure your face looks at the floor so your neck is straight.
▶ Hold for 10 seconds, then repeat on the other side.

How to be a woman travelling alone

... and enjoy your trip even more as a result

24

The idea of going it alone on a big trip is daunting for anyone and perhaps more so for women, for whom safety issues can be more of a concern. Don't let this put you off. Travelling solo, whatever your gender, opens up a whole world of new experiences as you navigate situations on your own, forge unusual friendships and basically do whatever you want whenever you want. Empowering as it might be, however, it's worth bearing the following tips in mind to ensure your trip goes smoothly.

1 Plan ahead, so you know what you should be wearing, so you avoid arriving in a new place late at night, so you always have enough money on you, and so on.

2 Read up on what is culturally acceptable and what is not. This way you avoid drawing attention to yourself for all the wrong reasons.

3 Having done your reading, use the same safety rules you do at home and trust your instinct: if you are comfortable you know what's happening, nothing beats female instinct for keeping you safe.

4 Know why you have decided to travel alone and be happy with that decision as this will help you with the many hundreds of decisions you'll make on your trip, from where you go to who you decide to engage with. And take that positive mindset with you: it will open so many doors.

Imogen Hall, travel writer

Street food smarts

Navigate the world's dazzling array of street food while keeping an eye on your health

▶ Give yourself a few days to adjust to the local cuisine, especially if you're not used to a commonly used ingredient or spice. You can always work up to the more unusual specialities over several days.

▶ You know the rule about following a crowd – if the locals are avoiding a particular vendor, you should too. Also take notice of the profile of the customers – any place popular with families will probably be your safest bet.

▶ If the vendor is cooking in oil, have a peek to check it's clean. If the pots or surfaces are dirty, there are food scraps about or too many buzzing flies, don't be shy to make a hasty retreat.

▶ Don't be put off when you order some deep-fried snack and the cook throws it back into the wok. It's common practice to partly cook the snacks first and then finish them off once they've been ordered.

▶ Unless a place is reputable (and busy), it's best to avoid eating meat from the street. As already noted, follow the crowds.

▶ The hygiene standard at juice stalls in many parts of the world is wildly variable, so exercise caution. Have the vendor press the juice in front of you and steer clear of anything stored in a jug.

▶ Don't be tempted by glistening pre-sliced melon and other fruit, which may keep its luscious veneer with the regular dousing of (often dubious) water. Buying fruit whole and peeling it yourself with a knife you've cleaned yourself is a good way forward.

Go vegan on the road!

Try out these vegan-friendly destinations, thanks to Drea Duclos ohdeardreablog.com

Country	What to say	Tuck in	Top tip
UK	Vegan versions of vegetarian or other mains can increasingly be prepared on request, so don't be shy to ask	Salads, veggie stews, beans on toast	Honey is often used on breakfast granola and porridge
Mexico	Specify *sin queso* (without cheese) on pretty much any dish that you order	Vegan takes on Mexican classics such as nachos, chilli and *mole*	Look out for *asiento o manteca*: pork lard sometimes used in tortilla and bean-based dishes
France	*Pouvez-vous préparer un repas vegan?* – 'Can you prepare a vegan meal?'	Look out for new openings in big cities where the emphasis is on seasonal produce	The word *végétalien* is also used to refer to vegan-friendly products on food packaging
India	Referring to a vegan-friendly religion such as Jainism can help when specifying what you will and won't eat	Curries, stews, dhal, thoran, the list is endless!	It can be hard to tell what is truly vegetarian or vegan – ghee and yoghurt are often used in cooking

Country	What to ask for	Tuck in	Top tip
Indonesia	*Saya tidak makan daging* – 'I will not eat meat,' doesn't cover all vegan bases but is useful nonetheless	Tempeh, rice, tofu, noodles, and many vegetable dishes	Be specific about what you won't eat. Using a list when ordering is fine
Jamaica	Ask Rastafarians where's good to eat. Many follow an Ital diet, which is close to vegan	A huge variety of fresh fruit, rice, beans and plantains are staples of the Caribbean table	Honey is sometimes used in sauces and marinades
USA	Checking what you're eating doesn't contain milk or egg is a smart move if ordering in a restaurant that isn't solely vegan	In vegan hot spots, such as the Californian cities, you'll have the choice of world-beating options	Vegan options can be limited outside of the big cities
Morocco	*Makanakūlsh lhem/makla lī fihā halīb* – 'I don't eat meat/dairy products'	Veggie *tagine*, couscous, olives, meat-free *harira* soup	Be warned: not all 'vegetable' dishes are necessarily meat-free

AVOID PITFALLS

How to turn rainy seasons to your advantage

Have a great trip, avoid the crowds of the dry season – and even get a tan

Common wisdom holds you shouldn't travel in the rainy season. It will be wet, and who wants a soggy holiday? But before changing plans, it pays to look a little closer. Thailand's rains, for instance, often come at night and leave quiet beaches and blue skies by day.

Chris McIntyre, Managing Director of Expert Africa (www.expertafrica. com), advises, 'Come in the dry, and you'll see animals around waterholes, but vegetation is sparse and there's not much going on.

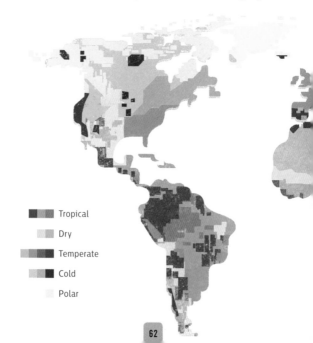

Tropical

Dry

Temperate

Cold

Polar

Come when the rains start and you'll experience everything coming to life, which is truly magical.' Of course, some sights, like waterfalls, are at their most dramatic during the wet season.

Cost is also a good reason to travel at monsoon time. Some camps may close, but those that stay open can offer terrific value. Lower demand can also mean that what would be peak season elsewhere, like July and August in India, is an affordable – if hot and sticky – time to travel.

The secret is to look very closely at your destination's weather patterns – microclimates can change things from one region to the next – and speak to locals and travellers who have been before you.

Complain well

Don't be shy
Don't forget you've paid a lot of money for your flight, experience or hotel room. If something's not right, speak up. Travellers are great at moaning, but not so good at raising complaints.

Speak up early
Travel firms want to deal with problems promptly. If something's not right, say so then. If it's raised later, it can be harder to make amends.

Get social
Customer service departments now monitor social networks, Twitter in particular, and are quick to respond to problems. Sign up before you go and follow the relevant accounts to speed things up.

Keep calm and carry on
Being angry is not the right way, no matter the issue. Be polite, but firm. You'll be taken more seriously if you don't act like a ranting maniac.

Consider writing a letter
A well-written letter, especially one showing a sense of humour, gives you room to make a point and will have a big impact if it gets in front of the right people. Keep copies of all correspondence.

EU airline compensation rules
Flying within, to or from the EU? It pays to know your rights as you could be entitled to compensation in the event of delays or cancellation. See the EU website for more details.

Ingrid Stone, author of Letters of a Dissatisfied Woman
(www.complaintsqueen.com)

What to look for in a travel insurance policy

Get yourself covered

29

Travel insurance will hopefully be something you don't have to worry about when travelling – but it is certainly something you need to sort out before you leave. Cover can be hard to arrange once you're on the road. Book with a reputable insurer before leaving home.

Be covered for where you're going
This sounds obvious, but check that your cover will apply where you're going, especially if you're visiting popular destinations just outside what may be considered Europe, such as Morocco and Turkey.

And for what you're doing
Attempting to ski? Going rock climbing? Diving? Make sure your cover extends to that. Read the policy carefully to see if there are restrictions relating to, for example, going off-piste. Best of all, plan ahead before you go to be sure you're covered for any activity you might take.

How much cover?
It may seem like your medical provision amounts to mind-boggling millions that you will never need, but remember this is worst-case-scenario stuff. As dramatic as it sounds, imagine the cost of you having to be medically repatriated. The highest levels of cover are worth it if you're going to the USA, where health care is expensive.

Take your documents – and a copy
Travel with your insurance documents, and also have a copy on email. Make sure you store the contact number of your insurer in your phone.

Drinking and insurance don't mix
Certain policies will be invalid if you are drunk or under the influence of drugs, so go easy when on the road.

Classic honeymoon fails and how to avoid them

Make sure your first trip as a married couple is as perfect as you've planned

30

That beautiful beach and just you and your newly betrothed. Bliss, right? Hopefully. But honeymoons are surprisingly easy to get wrong. Here's how to get off to a long life together on the right track.

Plan together
It's tempting for one of you to take on planning the honeymoon while the other books the band and caterer. Plan together and you're more likely to get what you both want from the trip.

Beach blues
Organising a wedding can be stressful. While the idea of flopping on a beach might appeal, it may prove harder to switch off than if you start with something urban or active for a few days to wind down. That said, a little luxury to start things off rarely strikes the wrong note.

Go for your dream honeymoon
If you've always dreamed of lemur-spotting in Madagascar or kayaking in Alaska together then you've got the perfect excuse to go. Just because the beach break is the stereotypical honeymoon doesn't mean it is right for you.

Travel as a gift
Friends love to contribute to your honeymoon in lieu of a toaster or set of teaspoons. Many travel companies – and some dedicated services – offer wedding registries that make great alternative gifts.

Once you're away
Adopting a new surname post-wedding? Make sure any bookings you make before getting hitched match the name on your passport.

An upgrade or two?

OK, so most honeymoons aren't paved with endless upgrades, but dropping into conversations at airport and hotel check-in desks, and in fact most places offering you a service is a good idea. You're only on honeymoon once – you might just find it opens a door or two, or gets something additional thrown in along the way.

Further reading

There's a world of great ideas out there – see sites like www.101honeymoons.co.uk and The Honeymoon Project (thehoneymoonproject.com), and Lonely Planet's *The Honeymoon Handbook* for all manner of honeymoon ideas.

How to avoid first-time cruise fails

**Q&A with Carolyn Spencer Brown,
Chief Content Strategist, Cruise Critic**

31

How has cruising changed in the past 15 to 20 years?
Cruises have been transformed over the past two decades. As
well as big-name ships with headline-grabbing facilities which
showed people – rather than told them – that cruising was fun,
the best cruises place emphasis on the destination as much as the
experience of life at sea. In my role I spend a huge amount of time
learning about and advising people on the possibilities of small- to
medium-sized cruises and expedition-style ships, where the focus is
on where you're going and what happens once on dry land.

**What are some of the common mistakes first-time cruisers make
when booking?**
Buying a cruise based on price alone is the single biggest mistake.
You should be looking to marry your own travel interest and lifestyle
with a cruise line and what they're offering. If you save $50 a day and
end up on a cruise that doesn't match your interests and doesn't go
anywhere you want to go, then that's a massively false economy.

**What questions should you ask to tailor a cruise to your
specific needs?**
It can be hard when starting planning as websites and brochures
can make it hard to tell the difference between individual cruises
and operators. The principal differences are in ship sizes, what
destinations are called at – and for what period of time – and the
experiences offered on and off the ship. This is one area of travel
when going to an agent who knows their stuff will pay dividends.
Ask lots of questions and think about what and where you're
interested in. A cruise specialist will be able to suggest things you
may not have thought of based on your taste, budget and the time
of year you're travelling.

What should you look for in terms of extras (eg flights, vehicle transfers, excursions) when booking?

The biggest misnomer about cruises today is that a cruise is all inclusive. They're not and this can catch people out. Activities, excursions and gratuities will all generally cost extra so it's important to plan for this. One way to save money is to look for companies – both agents and cruise lines – that offer a chance to bundle some of this together.

Is there anything unusual you should pack?

Cruising has become less formal but there are still dress codes on most ships, though levels of enforcement vary. Check when you book. Most ships are built to US power specifications so an adapter is useful. Cruise ship libraries have been pared back in many cases, so an e-reader or tablet loaded with books is a smart idea. Reliable, affordable wi-fi is not yet standard on cruises – though this is set to change in the next few years.

An expert's advice on train travel

In contrast with booking a flight, which is pretty much the same experience anywhere in the world, when taking a train you are almost immediately dealing with specific issues relating to where you're travelling to. This isn't a problem in the likes of Canada or Australia, where you can easily plan cross-country journeys, but in Europe it can make for a fragmented booking experience. In Europe, start with Deutsche Bahn (www.bahn.de) for timetable information and loco2.com or www.trainline.eu for bookings.

Point-to-point fares are almost always easier to book and better value than a railpass. The exceptions to this are if you are under 26, want flexible travel dates and are planning on covering long distances. Look out for quotas for passholder places on some trains, notably those to or within France.

High-speed routes needn't mean missing out on the best bits – many high-speed trains only travel on fast lines for part of the route, slowing down for trickier or more interesting bits. Do check if there's a slice of the journey you have your heart set on. Trains

down the Rhine aren't much slower than the high-speed routes that bypass one of Europe's loveliest train rides.

Try to maximise daytime travel for the best views en route. This doesn't mean missing out on sleepers, which remain one of the most romantic forms of travel and save a hotel bill to boot. Many routes will cover scenic stretches in the morning, such as the journey from Belgrade to Bar.

"High-speed routes needn't mean missing out on the best bits – many high-speed trains only travel on fast lines for part of the route, slowing down for the trickier or more interesting bits."

Generally, the earlier you book, the less you'll pay. You can book up to 11 months in advance in Australia, the US and Canada, 120 days in advance in India and in most of Western Europe. Watch out for discount fares going on sale at other times – check your destination's national rail website.

Mark Smith, founder of train travel website www.seat61.com

Avoiding theft and scams

Thieves prey on the unsuspecting, so get clued up to stay safe

Firstly, adopt an anti-scam mindset in everyday life so it's second nature when travelling. This means you don't have to adjust your behaviour on the road. For instance, don't let your credit card out of your sight in restaurants and avoid putting your phone on tables in pubs and cafes where it's easily snatched. On alfresco terraces especially, don't leave your bag (or jacket with anything in its pockets) hanging over the back of your chair.

Once travelling, one of the best ways to avoid being targeted is to blend in as much as possible. Wear clothes that are worn by locals in the region (that is, no shorts and Hawaiian shirts in Paris), don't walk around with a camera on show and avoid opening maps – duck into a cafe to read them discreetly, or use navigation on your phone with an earpiece.

Learning a phrase in the local language, such as 'Saya tinggal di Bali' – 'I live in Bali' (or the equivalent for whichever destination), has an amazing effect on dispelling nefarious types.

Have a handbag/carry bag with interior pockets so your wallet can't easily be lifted even if people manage to reach into your bag. Wearing your bag across your body also stops it being easy to swipe.

Catherine Le Nevez, Lonely Planet author and travel writer

AVOID
PITFALLS

Scams to watch out for

**Repeat the mantra: it's too good to be true,
it's too good to be true...**

While you're often safer overseas than you are in your hometown,
a few scams seem to pop up all over the world.

▶ **The scam: fake police**
Sometimes also real police, they'll demand to see your passport,
find something wrong with your visa and then suggest your
troubles will be over if you pay a fine. To them. In cash. Right now.

What to do: stand your ground and offer to accompany them to the
station. This will usually see the error 'excused'.

▶ **The scam: gem or carpet deals**
On entry into a store, often prompted by an enthusiastic taxi
or rickshaw driver, you will be offered a deal so preposterously
lucrative that refusing seems unthinkable.

What to do: think again – those gems are going to be worthless and
the carpet you buy probably won't make it home at all. There are
legitimate traders selling both jewels and rugs, and they don't act
like this.

▶ **The scam: bird poo**
The surprising splat of bird shit landing on you from a great height
is followed by the swift appearance of a stranger (or group of
individuals) offering a towel-down. In the confusion, valuables are
removed from your person, never to be seen again.

What to do: move fast. If you seem to have been the victim of a
bird strike, keep moving away from the area and avoid any offers
of help.

Surviving a small group tour

**Advice for feeling empowered, not imprisoned
by Emma Sparks, Deputy Editor, lonelyplanet.com**

Stay curious

With a tour company handling the travel logistics, it's easy to switch into 'passenger mode', which can be a treat, so long as you're not totally clueless about the itinerary. Do your destination research in advance, as you would for any independent trip (yes, even get a guidebook if you're so inclined), so that you don't spend the entire time playing catch up. Ask your guide lots of questions for extra context and recommendations – you can't beat insider knowledge!

Befriend your guide

Communicating effectively with your guide can take your tour to the next level. Ensure they are aware of any basic needs or issues (such as dietary requirements, travel sickness, allergies) so they can help you stay healthy and happy. Explain your goals for the tour – be it trying as many new foods as possible, exploring local architecture or finding an authentic souvenir – and a decent guide will make it happen. Finally, it's in everyone's best interest to listen closely to briefings.

Go with an open mind

All kinds of travellers take small group tours, so leave your preconceptions at the airport. You'll probably be mixing with an international crowd of varying ages and personalities, all of whom have different experience levels and definitions of what it means to travel. Be patient with your fellow voyagers and take the opportunity to hear their perspectives on the place you're exploring together – you could end up making friends for life.

Don't follow the crowd

There's going with the flow and there's staying in a dive bar for a fifth slippery nipple when all you really want is your bed. Don't feel pressured into sticking with your travel buddies 24/7 – alone time is a healthy way to punctuate what can be an intense group dynamic. If you need a rest, skip the morning activity and enjoy a lazy brunch, or eat at a food stall of your choosing rather than the group-friendly restaurant.

Take pocket money for extras
Study your tour inclusions closely and budget for any missing meals or optional activities. Unexpected expenses (or splurges) can crop up, so having a cash stash for those 'oh go on then' moments can prevent FOMO on the road. Many tour guides and drivers rely hugely on tips – if you think they've done a great job, be generous.

Overcoming loneliness

Five tips for beating the solo travel blues   36

1 Treat yourself
Once in a while stay at a nice hotel, or book yourself into a spa. Enjoy the moment and carry on feeling refreshed and energised.

2 Make a list
Refocus your energy on the task at hand. Why are you on this trip? Trade loneliness for ambition and write out a plan of action.

3 Connect with loved ones
Sometimes hearing a familiar voice is enough to cheer you up.

4 Sweat it out
There's nothing like an exercise-triggered endorphin rush to make you feel good about yourself.

5 Smile
A simple truth – smile and people will be more receptive to you.

Haggle like a master

If you're not having fun, you're doing it wrong

Haggling – or bargaining – is an essential part of everyday life in many countries around the world. It might not seem like it's for you at first, but remember it's a bit of a game, and not to be taken too seriously.

If you can, get the seller to name the price first. Then come back with 50% of that as your counter offer. The selling price – which will be a combination of the cost of the goods to the seller and their profit – will be somewhere in the middle of these two numbers. From here on it's a (good natured) battle of wills between the two of you.

Remember, you can start haggling for an item without being obliged to buy, but it's bad form to pull out if the seller comes down to your suggested price. If the price isn't satisfactory, feel free to walk away, or try your luck in another shop. In fact, walking away is a useful technique; if you're not called back by the seller then you were probably a long way off getting a price you both could have settled on. A little role-play can help too: feigning hurt or shock is all part of the game.

What time of day you shop can also influence your success. For many merchants a positive transaction with the first customer of the day is seen as a lucky omen, so they may take a lower price than they would once trading is underway. Conversely, if you visit at the end of trading, sellers may be willing to offer a discount to secure one last sale for the day.

Consider asking for another item to be thrown in to seal the deal. Sometimes, if you're haggling at an advanced level, this may be the item you wanted all along and the original item you're bidding on is the semi-desirable add-on.

Above all else, don't get stressed. The increment you're trying to shave off the price will probably not add up to much for you, but can make quite a difference to the seller. Have some fun but don't get mad chasing a price that may be a bad deal for the seller; the idea is for the dance to finish with both tango-ers feeling satisfied with the transaction.

Joe Bindloss, Destination Editor at Lonely Planet

How to travel with friends

... and not want to kill them   38

Set expectations
Discuss your general vision of the trip. Urban exploration? Beaches? If one person is a go-go-go type and the other is a chill-at-sidewalk-cafes type, friction will quickly arise. Carefully consider what you'd like to accomplish on your trip and communicate this.

Establish a budget
Unfortunately money (and how to spend it) is often the last straw for many strong relationships. Before you start planning, establish each other's comfort preferences and available funds for things like accommodation, food and transport.

Divide and conquer
It's perfectly fine to split up when you'd each prefer to do other things. Resentment grows quickly when one person is made to feel like they are catering to the other person's itinerary too frequently. Equally, splitting up, whether it's for three hours or three days, will soothe mounting frustrations.

DO THE RIGHT THING

Alternatives to flying

Don't want to fly? Here are some suggestions to get your plane-free adventure off the ground

39

Set sail

Of course there's no need to fly if you're on a cruise. Very different to a cruise, cargo ships offer a unique and green alternative to flying. Several shipping firms are happy to bring a limited number of passengers along for the ride. Journeys on freighters aren't cruises by any stretch of the imagination. Passengers are left to their own devices to while away the days, and mealtimes are simple affairs, taken with the crew.

"The option of overlanding by motorhome, car or even foot is undergoing something of a renaissance"

Take to two wheels

More and more intrepid travellers are experiencing the joys of bicycle touring, which in many countries requires little more than riding off from your front door. By taking your bike on a train or ferry you can reach interesting destinations further from home. See bikepacking.com for more info.

Sleep on the move

The option of overlanding by motorhome, car or even on foot is undergoing something of a renaissance as road conditions improve. Overland trucks still ply many backpacker routes around the world, and though you'll generally have to fly there and back, the journey in the middle remains one mighty adventure. When going inter-city, sleeper buses and comfortable *coche cama* buses found in South America offer a flight-free way to while the night away, as do sleeper trains.

Find a bona fide eco-hotel

How to find out if a hotel is as green as it's making out

40

From emerging niche to mainstream trend, hotels and resorts with green practices at the heart of their operations are now the norm rather than the exception. Going green can help a hotel save money by cutting energy and water use and reducing the amount of waste going to landfill. Using local produce is also increasingly recognised as being a cheaper option in many cases, and generally has the added benefit of being seasonal and organic. In theory this means choosing to stay somewhere that's genuinely eco-conscious should be straightforward, but standards do vary.

Start on the hotel website

Look for an environmental policy, and statements on social responsibility too. These shouldn't be tucked away but weaved through information about the hotel. See if the hotel has been certified by an awards scheme that sends experts to verify a hotel's claims, like the Tourism for Tomorrow Awards (wttc.org/tourism-for-tomorrow-awards). National certification schemes that have been accredited and are able to make like-for-like comparisons are also good indicators. All this allows you to build up a matrix-like view of a property's record on environmental and social responsibility.

Ask questions

Though decisions about where to stay are generally made before you arrive it's a great idea to keep asking questions once you're there. This not only shows that visitors value hotels and resorts investing in eco-friendly practices, but also gives staff a chance to talk about what their employer is doing. Green credentials are often a source of pride. Good eco-hotels use off-grid energy (like solar panels and wind turbines), thick insulation (eg double-glazing), low-energy light bulbs and keycards that control the room's electricity, air-con and heating.

"Good eco-hotels use off-grid energy (like solar panels and wind turbines), thick insulation, low-energy light bulbs and keycards that control the room's electricity"

What to look for

A sure sign that a hotel limits water usage is if it uses flow-restrictors in its taps and showerheads, and has dual-flush toilets. Keep an eye out for refillable pump dispensers in the bathroom instead of wasteful packets of plastic miniatures.

Richard Hammond, Founder and Executive Producer of Greentraveller Productions

Avoiding offence

How to stay on the right side of everyone as you travel

41

It's fairly difficult to cause so much offence as to get you into trouble. Generally, people you meet will be tolerant and understanding. The exceptions are if you offend local religious sensibilities, especially in stricter Islamic countries, or voice unpopular views about the government or royal family of the country you're in.

Do:

▶ Learn some local phrases, including 'excuse me', 'thank you' and 'I'm sorry' and air them when you need to.

▶ Follow the lead of those around you: if others are removing shoes or donning headscarves, do the same. Be especially watchful in religious buildings and sacred places.

▶ Smile! You'll find far more people ready to forgive the foibles of a visitor than those who take permanent offence.

▶ Leave your own perceptions of what's OK at passport control. In many Mediterranean destinations you'll be kissed several times on the cheek, whereas puckering up with someone you've just met in the USA should be replaced with a handshake. Reading up on greeting etiquette before you arrive will save many an embarrassed face.

▶ Be wary of using hand gestures – they can mean very different things depending where you are. Even the seemingly innocuous thumbs-up sign is considered rude in Egypt and Iran.

Don't:

▶ Emulate your fellow tourists' bad habits – scribbling your name on ancient monuments is not cool. Likewise, leave the padlocks off that bridge. It looks better without them.

▶ Take what might appear to be a local litter problem as an excuse to drop your own trash.

▶ Take pictures at sensitive military, religious or political spots and gatherings, including demonstrations.

▶ Assume that space you're taking a photo or selfie in is yours and yours alone, and watch where you're putting that selfie stick.

▶ Get into water when you're dirty. In many destinations, including Iceland and Japan, washing thoroughly before entering public bathing and swimming areas is compulsory. Which should be the case everywhere, when you think about it.

IF IN DOUBT, ASK A LOCAL

If you're worried about making a cultural faux-pas, connect with a local for guidance. But what if you don't know any locals or can't crack the language barrier? Many cities offer tours and experiences with locals who can show you how the place ticks. And if you'd like to stay in a local's home, sites like Couchsurfing (www.couchsurfing.com) can broker a night on someone's floor or sofa. Hosts are used to giving the inside track on their home city, and you'll feel more confident in no time.

World tipping chart

Get up to speed with the tipping etiquette of your destination – customs vary the world over

Destination	Restaurants	Bars	Taxi Drivers	Notes
USA	15-20%	$1 a drink minimum	10-15%	Tipping is not optional. Only withhold tips in cases of outrageously bad service
France	10%	Table service adds small tip of 10-15%	10-15%	The note *service compris* on your bill means service has been included in the price
Australia	5-10%	Not expected	Round up by a dollar or two	
Thailand	Rounding up	Change	50-100B	
New Zealand	5-10%	5-10%	Round up to nearest dollar	Your tour group leader will happily accept tips
UK	10-15%	Not expected unless food is ordered at table	10% or round up to nearest pound	
Spain	Service is charged by law: optional 5-10% on top	No established rule, small change	Round up to nearest euro	
India	10-15% optional	Unusual to tip	Can tip honest drivers	'Baksheesh' can loosely be defined as a 'tip'; it covers everything from alms for beggars to bribes
Italy	10% optional	Small change	Round up to nearest euro	

DO THE
RIGHT THING

Destination	Restaurants	Bars	Taxi Drivers	Notes
Egypt	10–15%	LE5-10 is customary in cafes	Round up the fare or offer 5% extra	
Morocco	10%	10%	Round up	Tipping a small amount is customary for many tourist services
Czech Republic	10%	5-10% for table service	Not expected, but rounding up is common	
Germany	5-10%	5%	5-10%	
Turkey	10%	10%	Round up to nearest lira	
Cuba	10%	CUC$1 per visit not per drink	10%	
Netherlands	Up to 10%	Up to 10%	Round up by 5%	
Vietnam	5%	Not expected	Not expected but appreciated	
Canada	15-20%	$1 per drink	10-15%	
Japan	Not customary	Not customary	Not customary	
Ireland	10-15%	Uncommon unless table service is provided, then €1	10%	

Tips for travelling plastic-free

Be part of the solution, not the problem

43

Travel anywhere and you'll see the impact our plastic habits have had on the world's landscapes and oceans. Beth Terry, creator My Plastic Free Life (https://myplasticfreelife.com), offers some suggestions for adopting a plastic-free travel style.

▶ Take a reusable bottle of water. Bring it through security empty and fill it up in the departure lounge. If you bring a double-walled container you can also use this for hot drinks both on the plane and on the ground.

▶ Bring your own food and utensils to avoid using the throwaway items commonly used on aircraft. Chances are it'll taste a lot better, and you can eat at times that suit you too. Pillows and blankets often get thrown away by airlines, so again, bring your own and travel with layers of clothing for varying temperatures. Your own headphones often work better than the ones you're given on a plane.

▶ If you pack tea and coffee, you won't need to use the pods offered in hotels. Toiletries in solid form will also last a trip and beyond. Those food containers you used on the plane can be useful for leftovers or any takeaway food items.

▶ Do your homework so that when you're on the ground somewhere new, you're clued up about local recycling and other waste disposal schemes. That said, a better approach is to avoid using single-use disposable items in the first place. Canvas shopping bags are easy to carry and versatile, and can carry anything you need for the day.

▶ Remember: you're a responsible citizen in your own neighbourhood, so you should be a responsible citizen in the place you're visiting. You're in someone else's home. Be a good guest.

DO THE
RIGHT THING

How to interact ethically with wildlife

The golden rules of responsible wildlife watching

44

Watching wildlife is a key reason to travel. However, many of the interactions travellers have with animals are on our terms, not those of the animal. How can we make sure our animal interactions are as ethical as possible? Kate Nustedt from World Animal Protection (worldanimalprotection.org.uk) offers some suggestions.

▶ The simple rule is that if you're invited to hug, stroke or ride an animal then there's some degree of cruelty involved. Generally the best way to experience an animal in their natural habitat is to keep a respectful distance.

▶ Use your power as a traveller. If you find yourself in a place where you're invited to an animal show, or otherwise get close to an animal when there's cruelty involved, then tell others about it, write online reviews and get on social media.

▶ The travel industry, both in home markets and destinations, is rapidly changing as consumers' awareness levels regarding the treatment of animals and expectations of high standards grows. Choosing a responsible operator is key. Go with one that respects animals and won't get involved in scrapping with others for the best viewpoints if you're on something like a safari.

▶ If you're swimming or snorkelling with wild dolphins or other creatures, remember that it is up to them if they approach you or not. A responsible operator will brief you on this.

▶ Forget selfies with animals. In case you're in any doubt, it's never really okay to cuddle a wild animal, even one that's ended up in a sanctuary.

Kate Nustedt, Global Wildlife Director, World Animal Protection (worldanimalprotection.org.uk)

Spend your money wisely

▶ If you're keen on travelling responsibly, then spending wisely is one of the key aspects of getting it right. It helps to think of your spending as an investment in the local community that you're temporarily a part of.

▶ Eating and drinking is a great opportunity to allocate your spend sensibly. Aim for smaller local stores, bars and restaurants. Local or family-run small guesthouses make a great alternative to chain hotels with far less character.

▶ Using public transport or hiring a bike means you'll be travelling in a way that will help you meet the people who live where you are visiting. It will mean there's one less car on the road and it's cheaper and more fun than a hire car.

▶ Aim for local markets when stocking up on produce, and try items that are sourced from the area you're in. This maximises the chances of local sellers and producers benefiting from your stay.

DO THE
RIGHT THING

▶ Souvenirs should also be locally made and distinctive. Seeking these out can be a lot of fun and might take you to artisan markets or boutiques that have an unusual selection of items.

▶ Steer clear of souvenirs made from protected or endangered animal or plant types and anything that appears to be a part of a country's unique heritage, such as ancient books or objects. Not only do these purchases encourage a trade in such objects, you might find that attempting to export them, as well as bringing them to your home country, requires a permit or is against the law.

> "Eating and drinking is a great opportunity to allocate your spend sensibly. Aim for smaller local stores, bars and restaurants. Local or family-run small guesthouses make a great alternative to chain hotels with far less character."

▶ As much as what you buy, hitting the right price point is important. Although bargaining too hard is no fun for anyone, paying too much might distort the market. Ask around to try to work out a fair ballpark price in advance.

▶ Do your research in advance to identify local guides who can add something to your experiences. Staff at your accommodation can often make recommendations, or you can try online at sites including www.vayable.com and www.embark.org. The best guides will cost a little more but this often ensures fair pay and a higher quality of experience.

ENJOY EVERY MINUTE

Year-round trip planner

Where to go when, whatever your travel style

	January	February	March	April	May	June
BEACH	East Coast Australia	Gambia	Cape Verde	St Lucia	Crete	Sardinia
ACTIVE	Skiing in British Columbia, Canada	Yachting in the Whitsunday Islands, Australia	Multi-sport adventure in Costa Rica	Snorkelling and scuba-diving, French Polynesia	Rock-climbing in the Lake District, England	Trekking the Andes, Peru
CULTURE	Temple-hopping, Thailand	Exploring Mughal forts and palaces, India	Colonial cities and music, Cuba	Vienna's museums and galleries, Austria	Old Kyoto, Japan	Art and architecture, Glasgow, Scotland
CITY	Prague	Cape Town	Beirut	Paris	Berlin	Reykjavik
HONEYMOON	Luxury *estancias*, Argentina	Castaway beaches, Maldives	Partying in Rio and rainforest adventures, Brazil	Jamaica's quiet coves	Country house escape, England	Spa hideaway and diving, Bali & Lombok
WILDLIFE	Rainforest adventures, Panama	Whales and seals, Península Valdés, Argentina	Orangutans, Borneo	Ningaloo Marine Park, Australia	Galápagos Islands, Ecuador	Wildebeest migration, Kenya & Tanzania

July	August	September	October	November	December
Ibiza, Spain	Cornwall, England	Fiji	Zanzibar, Tanzania	Florida Keys	Thailand
Via ferrata, Dolomites, Italy	Cycling the Wild Atlantic Way, Ireland	River running in the Grand Canyon, USA	Walking safari, Selous, Tanzania	Volcano boarding, Nicaragua	Skiing, Oregon, USA
Classical concerts and Imperial treasure, St Petersburg, Russia	Silk Road cities, Uzbekistan	Ancient history and modern art, Istanbul, Turkey	Old and new Rome, Italy	Morocco's Imperial cities	Dancing and dining, Buenos Aires, Argentina
London	Vancouver	Havana	New York	Auckland	Hong Kong
Open-top cruising, Italy	Tropical retreat, Mauritius	Five-star Paris	Namibia safari	Nile cruise, Egypt	Once-in-a-lifetime Australia
Brown bears, Alaska	Gorillas, Uganda & Rwanda	Reindeer, Lapland	Cave glow-worms, New Zealand	Lemurs, Madagascar	Penguins, Antarctica

Things an airline pilot knows about travel

Insider tips on getting from A to B

Pack smart

A large part of my job is about routine, and packing is no different. I have individual positions for each important item in my carry-on bag (passport, wallet, phone etc) so I know where to find it and, more importantly, whether it's missing.

Pick your timings

If travelling a primarily north or south long-haul route with few or no time zone changes, I highly recommend a daylight flight that departs in the morning. You'll arrive in the evening and have a good night's rest upon arrival, waking up fresh the next day. Doing the same flight overnight is a different story.

Be prepared

In the very unlikely event of an emergency, you need to be mobile and ready for anything. There's nothing wrong with taking your shoes off and changing mid-flight, but during take-off and landing always wear long pants and a good pair of shoes.

"I have individual positions for each important item in my carry-on bag so I know where to find it"

Stay hydrated

I don't leave home without lip balm: cracked lips and long flights go hand in hand. For long-haul flights I can't stress enough the importance of hydration, not just during but before and after the flight. So avoid caffeinated drinks, as well as alcohol.

Andrew Pascoe, commercial pilot

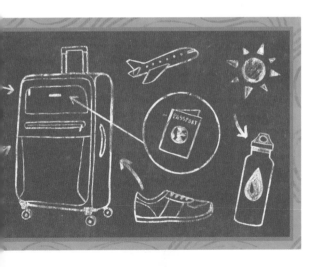

When you can't control the weather

Hit the town
Sunshine destinations revolve around good weather, but cities pretty much keep going regardless. If the weather's ropey, consider making an urban excursion and take advantage of museums and galleries.

Take refuge in culture
Seek out local cinema and theatre – the smaller the better. This is not only a chance to mug up on local culture (try going to the cinema in India for a wildly different experience) but if you're lucky you'll discover an interesting older building to boot. Libraries can be an unusual but welcome refuge. Many have free wi-fi, and any decent one will have a stash of locally themed books to immerse yourself in.

Wrap up and get active
Some outdoor activities (such as surfing) involve getting pretty wet anyway, so consider ways you can hit the beach even if things are inclement. A wetsuit will keep you warm for hours while messing around in the sea you should have pretty much to yourself. For active pursuits like hiking there's no need to pause if the weather's bad, only to make sure you've got the right gear. Consider packing a quick-drying travel towel if you're going somewhere it might be soggy.

Make the weather the star
Some buildings are enhanced by rainy weather. An example is the Pantheon in Rome, where visitors can see the surreal sight of rain streaming through the oculus (the hole in the roof) into a Roman temple, and then draining through the floor. And let's not forget places where stormy skies are the central attraction – the famous Catatumbo lightning storms over Lake Maracaibo in Venezuela even bring in tourists!

Oliver Smith, Travel Writer of the Year 2017/18

Curb your fear of flying

Keeping calm in the air

49

What if you don't want to get on the plane? Professor Robert Bor from the Centre of for Aviation Psychology offers some suggestions.

Know you're not alone
Estimates suggest 1 in 10 people on board an aircraft are not comfortable. The aviation industry spends a lot of time and

money finding ways to help everyone in the industry, from passengers to pilots, to combat psychological issues related to flying. This means there's lots of help available that's aimed at being practical and actionable.

Understand your fear
There is a difference, however, between people who have a state of apprehension about being on a plane, in a confined space or in an unfamiliar environment and those who have a phobic anxiety about flying. The approach you take will vary depending on the nature of your anxiety.

Ask for help
Your first port of call may be your doctor to discuss your concerns. Depending on what they say, different avenues can be explored. Many airlines around the world run excellent courses aimed at combating a fear of flying. These courses often explain something of the mechanics and aerodynamics of flying. Some people find seeking greater awareness can help. Others simply have other things going on in their lives that come out when they get on a plane, and in addressing these issues, perhaps through a psychologist, the anxiousness caused by flying recedes.

Keep it clean
In the lead up to flying take steps to keep as calm as possible. Avoid caffeine and alcohol, and fight any urge to skip meals. Try to arrive at the airport rested and relaxed. A few drinks to settle your nerves is not a good idea. It will initially act as a sedative, but once it wears off your original anxiety may well be amplified. Once on board, it may be useful to mention to the cabin crew that you're a nervous flyer, to practise deep breathing, and remember that statistically you are using what is by far the safest form of transport.

How to turn any business trip into a mini-break

Make the most of being somewhere new – even if you spend most of your time in an office

Use those jet-lagged hours
Strolling in the early hours can be magical, and make you feel like you're the only traveller in town. Some places, like markets, are at their best very early. You could even aim for a celebrated cross-town coffee shop for breakfast, giving you a slice of local life before your colleagues are ready to get down to work.

Look at listings before you travel
Getting tickets for a show or sporting event can be easier than you think, and often impresses your hosts. A spare ticket for a baseball match or concert rarely goes begging.

Make the most of down-time
Even the busiest schedules include spare hours, such as lunchtime or pre-dinner. Look into cycle-hire schemes that could allow you to whizz around and see something of the city.

Go for the big thing
One 'must-do' in the city? Make plans to see it with a colleague in advance of arriving. This can help to make it a more concrete part of your schedule when you might be tempted to drop it in favour of another working dinner.

Pro tip from Tom Otley, Editorial Director at Business Traveller
Pack your trainers: many larger hotels offer jogging maps with pre-planned routes around parks, traffic-free paths and even landmarks.

How a concierge can make your trip unstoppable

Think a concierge is only for wealthy business types? Think again.

51

Jose Pacuo, Head Concierge at the Milestone Hotel & Residences, London (www.milestonehotel.com), offers some suggestions on when a concierge can make the difference to your trip.

A good concierge is the gatekeeper to their city, and is the key to unlocking exactly the experiences a guest at their hotel is after. So they're a great place to start for personalised suggestions and advice on tours and outings. As they're specialists in their city, you can expect a pretty accurate and tailored piece of advice.

Concierges are engaged by guests in a variety of ways – from helping with basic necessities like finding a parking space or getting directions to planning the entire duration of a stay. If you have an unusual request, like trying to source a particular item as a gift back home, a concierge can save you time and help you find the best in class, and even arrange to buy it for you.

An experienced concierge won't be fazed even by unusual requests, so don't be shy in asking for their help. If they don't know the answer themselves they'll have an impeccable contacts book to find someone in the city who does.

Top tips for family fun while you travel

Make memories, not mayhem

Travelling with kids can be a stressful experience, but a little advance planning goes a long way towards making a happy holiday.

Know your audience
Understand what everyone in your family likes to do on holiday and create a plan around that. A 'boring' city break can be made into a great adventure if you find a brilliant playground near your apartment and don't stint on the ice cream.

Factor in down time
Trying to cram too much in is a sure fire way to make the family tensions rise so make sure each day has time for everyone to breathe

out. If you're going multi-generational, set the parameters early: not everyone has to do everything together all the time. Your teens will thank you for this.

Always carry snacks

You never know when you will be delayed, get stuck in a long queue, lose your wallet, miss the local restaurant's lunch time window. You can get through most things if you have snacks and water.

Get involved

The best thing about a family trip is the chance to spend time together without the pressures of daily life, so make the most of it. Play games, read about your destination together, try new things, write a diary together. Have fun, together. You're making the memories which will stay with you all for a lifetime.

Snag the hottest table

Hungry for a meal at that super-trendy place to eat? Learn the ways to sneak in even when it's fully booked

53

1 **Don't take no for an answer.** No-shows happen even at the coolest place in town, so calling on the day or turning up and asking isn't a lost cause. To show you're serious, tell them that you're prepared to wait.

2 **Sit at the bar.** Ask if there are communal tables or a spare seat or two at the bar rather than a fully booked table for two or four. Many restaurants are increasing capacity in these less-formal spaces as solo dining and a desire for a more relaxed meal grow in popularity.

3 **Dress up.** If you're being spontaneous, make sure you look the part. Someone who's smartly dressed at a smart location stands a better chance of being squeezed in than someone in shorts and trainers.

4 **Aim for unusual times of the day.** A very early or late sitting, or even breakfast, can be an easier time to score a table. If you're jetlagged, this might be a time that suits you better anyway. Take note of local peak-time dining periods, which vary hugely from country to country.

5 **Ask a local for help.** Ask a hotel concierge if they can swing something for you. Sometimes their local knowledge and contacts can open something up. If they do, make sure you tip them for their services (see p105 for more concierge guidance).

Adventure up your trip

Try a new approach to zing up your trip and throw up unexpected experiences

54

Is a destination not exciting enough for you? Adventurer and TV presenter Simon Reeve (simonreeve.co.uk) has some suggestions on how to add some spice to your vacation.

▶ Go out at night, and dawn. Exploring a new locale shouldn't be restricted to 9 to 5. There's always a surprise to be had watching a city after dark, or just as it's waking up.

▶ Ditch the big sights and instead take pleasure in detail. Draw a circle around your home base and explore the area forensically.

▶ Pore over local press. Forget international news and CNN. Nothing will immerse you in where you are like local news. If all you find is mundane then you can relish finding a rare, quiet part of the world.

▶ Camp. Even better, wild camp. It heightens your senses and brings you into closer contact with your surroundings.

▶ Travel randomly. Flip a coin at intersections and follow your nose.

Push the limits of your comfort zone

... and don't let fear rule the day

55

Travel and trying new things go hand in hand, but sometimes fear pops up and crushes your motivation. This simple three-pronged mindfulness task will help you get over the barrier.

1 First recognise the fear and admit the effects it has on you (panic, racing heart).

2 Next, ask yourself, what's the worst thing that can happen? You'd look silly? You'll fall in the water? It's usually all stuff you'd get past.

3 Remember if you *did* fail, there's at least one good thing: you'd never have to regret not having tried. Make a plan to start small and just do it.

Tips for your first ever digital detox

See the world beyond a phone screen

56

Travel and holidays are the perfect time to switch off from work and other pressures. You can't fully immerse yourself in a destination when you're being pulled back to your device every few seconds. And if you're distracted, you're less likely to enjoy yourself.

The benefits of switching off are likely to include better sleep, more focus, better concentration and even happiness. And we're not talking about switching off altogether, just making sure you use your devices in a smart way.

Start by moving social media apps and messaging services that consume your time or attention like work email either off your home screen, or off your phone altogether. Next, consider leaving your phone at home while you're out exploring or having dinner. Don't worry about not having a camera all the time – moments can be more memorable if you focus on them, rather than trying to capture them.

Consider getting a non-smartphone for trips. A non-internet enabled phone that takes calls and texts is also less attractive to thieves, and will keep your mind on where you are while still leaving you contactable.

You're not going to miss out. Everyone who's been on a digital detox trip said they felt like they missed nothing. The secret is to try ditching your device – the fear is really of what might happen.

Tanya Goodin, digital detox expert and author of OFF: Your Digital Detox for a Better Life *and* Stop Staring at Screens!

ENJOY EVERY MINUTE

Ten golden rules
of travel photography

Learn the art of snap-happy to achieve the best shots

57

1 **Take control of the picture-taking process.**
Get to know your gear and learn the technical stuff so you can take your camera off the automatic setting.

2 **Learn to see the transformative power of light.**
Understand how light translates onto the sensor, and be prepared to wait or return at the optimal time of day for shooting.

3 **Practise, practise, practise.**
Planning and executing a shoot of your own city is a great way to practise your skills and test your camera equipment.

4 **Research and plan.**
For the most productive and enjoyable time, ensure you have a plan and an understanding of the size and layout of the destination.

5 **Develop a picture-taking routine.**
A good routine, covering everything from timings and getting equipment ready, plays a big part in the success of your shoot.

6 **Be patient and commit to the image.**
Whether it's waiting for action to occur or the weather to change, a bit of patience can vastly improve the quality of your images.

7 **Pay for photos only when it's appropriate.**
A fair and reasonable exchange or a tiresome annoyance? If you do decide to pay, agree on the price beforehand, don't be afraid to bargain.

8 **Shoot raw files.**
To get the best results from your digital camera, use the raw file format. Adjustments such as exposure and contrast can be made later.

9 **Become proficient with image-editing software.**
Your investment in time and software will be rewarded with the ability to bring your images to life and have total control over how they look.

10 **Critique your photos objectively.**
Study your pictures to see what you did wrong and right. Next time you can eliminate the issues and concentrate on the things that worked.

See Lonely Planet's Best Ever Photography Tips *for more detail, and many more invaluable suggestions*

How to get the perfect Instagram shot

Bask in the glory of an impeccable feed

The angle
One of the best things about Instagram is that what constitutes the 'perfect shot' is pretty fluid. Due to the popularity of the channel among travellers, when it comes to capturing the world's iconic sights, someone (or many someones) will have got there first. So why not experiment? Is there a different angle of Angkor Wat, or a framing of Fez that you could capture? An imaginative angle often tells more of a story.

The crowds
Crowds are the eternal enemy of the Instagrammer, but are pretty unavoidable. Research the quietest times of day to visit your chosen shoot location (spoiler: these will largely be unfathomably early in the morning). Alternatively, consider using different shot perspectives to disguise the fact that there are crowds.

The lighting
Capturing atmosphere is key to nabbing the perfect travel shot. Lighting is one of the most malleable and influential tools at your disposal here – consider where you position its source in the frame. Backlit shots are good for drama, while images with the light source visible in them conjure a sense of freedom.

The format
Instagram offers options when it comes to what format you present your images in. A standard feed-post works best as a square, as it fills the largest amount of screen space when viewed on a phone or tablet. Try to avoid using landscape or portrait shots for feed posts where possible. Remember that you can also use Instagram's 'story' function for shots that are less standalone and work as a sequence.

Emily Frost, Lonely Planet's Social Communications Coordinator and serial Instagrammer

Capture the trip

Put pen to paper for an old-school memento 59

In a world of instant digital communication, a journal will document your trip in a uniquely personal and very different way. Here's how to create the perfect keepsake.

▶ There are plenty of custom-made travel journals out there but all you really need is a notebook of pretty much any kind. A hardback is helpful for giving you something to lean on and will protect against the rigours of being bashed about on a long trip.

▶ A journal acts as your memento and is not generally something that publishers will rush to put into print. You can, however, use the notes in it as a springboard for articles, blog posts and other stories.

▶ Try to commit to writing something every day. Even a few sentences before lights out will help you get down the key events. A journal is the perfect companion for a long journey or a solo meal.

▶ As well as your own words and sketches – a selection of coloured pencils is a fine accessory for a journal – consider using (or drawing) maps, and include ticket stubs, leaflets and even physical items, as well as notes from people you meet along the way. All of these will add to the richness of what you end up with.

▶ If travelling with children, keeping a journal can be a great downtime activity for them, as well as preserving their memories of fleeting experiences. It needn't simply be a diary, either – journal entries can take any form, including letters to friends at home, comics or memorable quotes the kids have heard along the way.

▶ If you're on a long trip, consider posting your journals home as you fill them up. This means there'll be no risk of losing them and they'll be waiting for you when you return.

Staying mindful on the road

Learning to relax and enjoy the present moment

Mindfulness, or the process of bringing one's attention to experiences happening in the moment, aligns perfectly with travelling. By focussing on what we are experiencing we get more out of the travel experience. Regular practitioners of mindfulness might consider travelling to a retreat as a great way to both develop their practice and experience a new destination, but if you're new to mindfulness, why not start with these simple tips:

Put your phone down
Nothing takes us out of the moment as much as the ping of a Whatsapp notification or scrolling through our Facebook feed. Set yourself a time limit and don't look at your phone for that period. See p112 for more tips on taking a digital detox.

Sit and watch the world go by

People watching is a fascinating activity wherever you are and an easy way to make yourself stop and take in your immediate environment. Bring your focus to the taste of your coffee, the sensation of the chair, the smell of the cafe.

Make a walk a wander

All too often we're in a rush to get somewhere, a rush to get something done and a rush to plan the next step. Being away is a chance to put a stop to all that. Take a walk without a purpose and let chance lead you.

When things go wrong, breathe

Travelling is stressful and there will be times when your heart rate is pumping. Breathing in for three counts, holding your breath for four and breathing out for five is a quick way to regulate adrenalin and allow your mind to focus.

Eat well while travelling...

... to get a true taste of your destination

61

Local menus and cuisine can be slightly bewildering at first, so how can you get the most out of the food scene in a new place?

Make one of your first stops a local market. As well as being lots of fun and somewhere you can feel part of everyday life, they're great places to stock up on money-saving self-catering options. Many cities with a foodie bent have guides offering market tours showcasing the local produce.

Ask for advice. Your local hotelier or host should be full of suggestions on where to eat – and don't forget to ask where they eat

too. Once you're there, putting yourself at the mercy of waiting staff and telling them you want what's good and fresh is always fun. Don't forget to tell them what your budget is.

A tip practised by power-lunching business travellers is to order two starters instead of a starter and a main. Tapas-style small plates are a good way to try lots of things without necessarily scoffing half of Spain.

Not every meal has to be a three-course blow-out. Consider sharing plates, going out for dessert and trying the local street-food scene to sample, little and often, the food that's good and distinctive.

Useful apps and websites for travellers

Our pick of digital tools to help you plan your trip and execute it flawlessly

---

62

▶ **SeatGuru and GateGuru**
A pair of wise apps aimed at making the end-to-end process of flying as easy as possible. Pair with Kayak or Skyscanner for booking flights.

▶ **Rome2Rio**
Directions to and from anywhere in the world, with transport options and prices.

▶ **XE**
All purpose currency converter website and app.

▶ **Citymapper**
Urban transport made easy wherever you are.

▶ **Hotel Tonight**
Short notice hotel-deals app.

▶ **Flush**
Crowd-sourced public convenience locator, with toilets around the world.

▶ **Accuweather**
Weather information for any destination in the world.

▶ **Government safety advice**
The websites of the US Consular Department (http://travel.state.gov), the UK Foreign & Commonwealth Office (www.fco.gov.uk) and the Australian Department of Foreign Affairs & Trade (www.dfat.gov.au) all offer up-to-date travel and safety advice.

▶ **LiveTrekker**

Is there someone at home who would kill to join you on your Himalayan hike? Now they can, thanks to this app that allows you to create a digital journal of your journey on an interactive map. You can add pictures, text, audio and video along the way, creating a multimedia travel diary you can share with whomever you like, whenever you like.

▶ **TouchNote**

This fun app allows you to send photos from your travels as physical postcards. Once you have selected your photo and message, TouchNote will print and post the cards for you – typically for a lower cost than you would pay in postage from your current destination.

▶ **LoungeBuddy**

This app aims to take some of the stress out of flying by letting you access those havens of peace and quietly clinking gin and tonics: the airport lounge. Plug in your itinerary and the app will let you know which lounges are at your disposal. If nothing turns up, you can pay a one-off fee to enter your lounge of choice. No membership or first class ticket required.

▶ **Tripcast**

Perfect for travellers who want to share every moment of their journey with loved ones at home, Tripcast allows you to create a photo album and invite friends and family to follow. They'll then be able to see every single photo that you post in real time, together with a location tag, and be able to 'like' and comment on images.

▶ **Lonely Planet** offers two useful free apps.
Guides is an indispensable on-the-ground tool for exploring cities.
Trips offers a simple way to share your travel experiences.

OVER
TO YOU

Over to you

Lonely Planet's community on social media is millions strong. We asked our Facebook group what their number one travel tip was. Here's a selection of their answers.

Take a picture of your luggage before checking it in. This makes it easier if it gets lost.

Angela Mallon

Travel with other people who are into your travel style.
Jamie Hs

Pay extra for skip the queue tickets!
Jim Descher

If available do a free walking tour.
Catherine Allaway

Don't flash your expensive camera/ mobile phone/ sunglasses/ clothing...!
Pierre-Luc Allard

Don't be afraid to go it alone.
Kristina Spears

Do your research on the place and have a flexible plan; ie, don't plan your trip hour by hour. Have a list of things you want to do and strike them out at your leisure.
Kyle Copeman-van Der Vlist

Start the trip with an empty mind, enjoy it and try to fill your mind with new things such as culture, language, cuisine and love.
Chiến Trần

Super comfortable shoes... It's the feet that travel and the eyes that see!
Sangeeta Tikekar

Don't wait for "one day". Go NOW!
Amy Griffey

Have hard copies of your documentation and scanned copies in your inbox.
Nelet Kok

Over to you

Make a plan but don't be afraid to deviate from it.
Paige Belford Authement

Learn even a little bit of the language the locals speak.
Robert Wilson

Always carry a small pack of wet wipes in your bag/purse. They clean up spills and dirty hands or just cools you down. It's also a great way to make friends by offering people one.
Mathilde de Gooijer

Roll your clothes when packing.
Emil Lundin

Carry spare set of clothes in waterproof bag.
Bryan Martin

My travel checklist

Notes

Notes

Index

Index

Acknowledgements

Published in November 2018
by Lonely Planet Global Limited
CRN 554153
www.lonelyplanet.com
ISBN 978 1 78701 764 1
© Lonely Planet 2018
Printed in China
10 9 8 7 6 5 4 3 2 1

Managing Director, Publishing Piers Pickard
Associate Publisher Robin Barton
Commissioning Editor Dora Ball
Art Direction Daniel Di Paolo
Illustration & Design Tina García
Editors Gabrielle Innes, Nick Mee
Print Production Nigel Longuet
Thanks Neill Coen, Emily Frost, Simon Hoskins

The biggest thanks go to the wide range of experts, writers and travel professionals who gave up their time to contribute to this book. I am very grateful to Dora Ball and everyone at Lonely Planet who's worked with me for being superb colleagues to work with on this book. Lastly, thanks to Imogen Hall for a world of help and support and to George, Harry and Winnie for the constant inspiration. Tom Hall

STAY IN TOUCH lonelyplanet.com/contact

AUSTRALIA
The Malt Store, Level 3, 551 Swanston St,
Carlton, Victoria 3053 T: 03 8379 8000

USA
124 Linden St, Oakland, CA 94607
T: 510 250 6400

IRELAND
Digital Depot, Roe Lane (off Thomas St),
Digital Hub, Dublin 8, D08 TCV4

UNITED KINGDOM
240 Blackfriars Rd, London SE1 8NW
T: 020 3771 5100